My Walk with God Continues

Life After Stroke

KIM BLACKWELL

MY WALK WITH GOD CONTINUES: LIFE AFTER STROKE

Bennett books may be ordered through booksellers or by contacting:

Bennett Media and Marketing
1603 Capitol Ave., Suite 310 A233
Cheyenne, WY 82001
www.thebennettmediaandmarketing.com
Phone: 1-307-202-9292

ISBN: 978-1-957114-40-8 (Paperback)
ISBN: 978-1-957114-41-5 (eBook)

Printed in the United States of America

TABLE OF CONTENTS

Book dedication

I dedicate this book to the teachers of the word of God in my life, Pastor Frederick Price Jr, Bishop Naomi Davis, and Reverend Venord Mark Cowan.

INTRODUCTION

When I was 51 years old, I was doing what I loved, which was running an art business and working with a travel company. On October 8, 2008, early in the morning, I had the worst headache that I ever had before in my life. I wouldn't be able to get to the hospital until 10 hours later. It was determined that I had suffered a massive stroke. The left side of my body was paralyzed, my peripheral vision became impaired and my speech slurred. I considered myself then to be pretty healthy because I worked out 3 times a week; I ate fish, chicken, and turkey and visited my doctor regularly.

All I could do was put my faith and trust in God and work hard to get better. My foundation scripture became Second Timothy 1-7, which says, "God has not given us a spirit of fear, but of power and love and of a sound mind". After 3 weeks in the hospital and 9 months of physical therapy, two months in California, and seven months in Philadelphia with family, I made a miraculous recovery.

Three neurologists looked at my brain MRI and said I should not have survived. When I returned to California, I was a different person. I had lost my identity and my independence. Who was I now? My foundation scripture became Philippians 3 13,14 which says "brethren, I do not count myself to have apprehended but one thing I do forgetting those things which are behind and reaching forward to those things which are ahead I press toward the prize of the upward call of God in Christ Jesus".

My brother suggested I write a book, that I had a great story to tell and I could help many people through my book. I took his advice; I wrote the book to share my story to help others avoid the unnecessary pitfalls that I experienced. Writing the book gave me a purpose, a subject that I am passionate about, and a new career. In 2017, "From Stroke to Recovery; My Walk with God, A guide to recovery was published".

Now, I am an author and a stroke survivor. It is only by the grace of God that there is life after a stroke for me. My walk with God means I walk by faith every day. I put my faith and trust in God and confess the word of God and act on it by faith. James 1,22 says; "be a doer of the word, not a hearer only deceiving yourselves". Romans 10,17 says; "faith comes by hearing and hearing by the word of God".

My foundation scripture for life after stroke is John 16-33, which says; "These things I have spoken unto you, that in me you might have peace, in the world, you shall have tribulation. But be of good cheer: I have overcome the world."

Life After Stroke Continues

In 2017, I was still having jerks and twitching of my left arm, hand and leg from the seizure that I suffered in 2009. I would stop them by praying in the spirit. My doctor's solution was to increase my medication. I had an HMO health insurance plan and sometimes there would be a lot of turnovers of doctors because either they were not paid well, live too far away or moved out of state. This time, it was my neurologist leaving and I got a new one; Dr. Brazil.

Philippians 4-19 says "God shall supply all your needs according to his riches in glory by Christ Jesus." On my first appointment, she said that I looked like I was falling asleep and I told her that I get up early. On the second appointment, she said the same thing, "you look like you're falling asleep". I thought to myself, "Is she asking me that again?". Her next question was,

"Do you snore?" and I said "yes, all my life". She says, "Kim, I think you may have sleep apnea. I would like you to take a sleep study test. I think this might have contributed to you having a stroke". The results of the sleep test were that, I stop breathing 20 times in one night. She put me on a CPAP machine. It took three machines before I found the right one for me. It's funny, when I told people that I had sleep apnea, it seemed like everyone had it.

After discussing that with Dr. Brazil, I decided to tell her about my jerking and twitching that I called small seizures. She said, "Kim, I do not think they are seizures because you have not had a big one since 2009. I think they are muscle cramps. I would like to put you on medication that we use with Parkinson's patients for restless leg syndrome." I thought to myself, "more medication?".

"Let's see if it works". She placed me on baclofen and pramipexole low dosages. It worked. In April, my girlfriend, Sharon asked me if I was ready for another dog. She said a lady from her church was looking for a good home for her dog because she had to move in with her children and they could not have pets. As they were on their way to bring the dog to me, Sharon said that KJ a.k.a. Kim's joy was acting up in the car with his owner and she was not sure he was going be the right dog for me.

But when he got here, we bonded right away, he was a cute three-year-old male Pekingese. He was house trained, loved to go for walks and was independent and could stay at home by himself with no problem. In 2018 I Had 2 book signing. One at my home and one at Simple Wholesome restaurant. I also had 2 speaking engagements.

In August, Michael and I with friends went to New Orleans to celebrate my 60th birthday and I had a great time. We called our vacation "The East Coast Tour". We went to Philadelphia to meet my family. Then to Patterson New Jersey to meet his family. Made a stop in New York and then headed to Washington DC for three days to visit the National Museum of African American history and culture. It was a wonderful experience.

African Americans have contributed so much to this country and I recommended that everyone go and visit the museum. We went back to Philadelphia for couple of days and then returned to California.

In 2019 Michael took me to the Monterey Jazz Festival a place that I've always wanted to go. Tammy went with me so that I could have someone to be with while Michael was working. We had a great time.

About the Author

Kim Blackwell is a stroke survivor! In 2008, she suffered a massive stroke; by defying the odds, she made a miraculous recovery. She put her faith and trust in God and worked hard to recover, knowing that God would see her through the challenges she would face to get her life back. In 2017, Kim published her first book, "From Stroke to Recovery; My Walk with God A Guide to Recovery." She wrote the book to tell her story and to help others avoid the unnecessary pit falls that she experienced.

She is a Christian woman who loves art, likes to travel, and enjoys the company of her dog, Princess. Ironically, she didn't seek to get a dog until after suffering a stroke but found them to be faithful friends! Her message to you is, "All things are possible if you put your faith and trust in God! Believe in yourself, be determined, persevere and never give up." Now, with her company, "My Walk with God" she shares information that inspires and motivates people who are in the process of illness recovery and who want to get their lives back on track.

She shares her efforts with others through public speaking and book sales. In this her new book, "My Walk with God Continues; Life After Stroke." Km Blackwell continues to tell her story because it was only by the grace of God that there was life after stroke for her. My walk with God is a life style of walking by faith and not by sight. She hopes her story encourages others to do the same. As with stroke your lifestyle is the only thing that we can control.

THE BOOK

I published my first book; "From Stroke to recovery; my walk with God" with a self- publishing company which is easy to do and I maintained control over everything. It has been a learning experience. I quickly learned that, there are illegitimate companies, scammers, and people who want to take advantage of you just like in any other business. I admit that I fell for a few, but God says he will never leave you nor forsake you and he is with you wherever you go. I believe that, trust that and I cast my cares on him and whenever I was in a situation where anything was taken illegally from me, I always get it back.

There have been many positive things that have happened though. I had an opportunity to be a co-author on a book titled, "Entrepreneurial Women of Faith". SHARING our anchor scriptures; we used to keep ourselves focused on and motivated in our businesses. I have been a guest on the following radio programs, "KJLH Front Page with Dominique Di Prima, Ric Bratton, This Week in America and Al Cole People of Distinction."

The book got good reviews on Amazon which opened the door for publishing companies and marketing firms to contact me. My goal was to get acquired by a traditional publishing company but I did not know the process. You have to have a literary agent who prepares everything they need to submit to the publishing companies.

I was blessed that my book was highly recommended by many people in the book industry. it is a long process with a lot of pieces to the puzzle. I got an offer that did not work out. So, I turned it over to God and I rest because I know that if it is supposed to happen it will. I wish nothing but success to all who have a story to tell. May God bless you throughout your journey.

My Soul Mate

I divorced in 1999 due to irreconcilable differences. That was a very difficult time for me because I had accepted Jesus Christ as my Lord and Savior. I focused on the word of God and applied it in my life, It changed me and healed my heart. I prayed and trusted that God would send the right man in my life. Isaiah 40:31 says; "But those who wait on the Lord shall renew their strength, they shall mount up with wings like eagles, they shall run and not be weary, they shall walk and not faint." In 2011,

God blessed me with Michael Phelps THE ARTIST. He is everything that I pray for and more. You never know what God is doing behind the scene. I Prayed for a black man, older but not too old. That he would like to travel and his kids would be grown. Finally, he would understand my health conditions and be able to handle my situation If I had another stroke, seizure or any other health issues.

Michael was one of my clients, his company name was 'Master Peace Collections'. Michael grew up in the South as a child, his family later moved north to Patterson New Jersey. He went into the military, after that moved to California. He worked at McDonald Douglas then left there and opened his own business.

He owned a retail clothing store. As an artist, he began creating shadow boxes with instruments inside. To market his product, he started doing art shows and festivals and was very successful. So, he closed the clothing store and focused his efforts and energy on his artwork.

Michael liked one of the artists that I represented; J Michael Howard. He created beautiful jazz themed 'oriented art'. Michael would buy his prints and frame them and sell them at his shows. He said that, he was always trying to ask me out but I was all about business. Michael heard that I was recovering from a stroke in Philadelphia, he called me every day to see how I was doing.

When I returned to California, I gave an art show at my home and invited Michael to participate. Later, he would tell me that he said that he was going to let me know how he felt about me. He said he was going to put it all out there. I had refreshments and at the last minute, decided to make ice tea. When he came and saw the ice tea, he said, "I love ice tea". Our chemistry was immediate. I knew that his love and concern for me was real.

My friends were there to witness the beauty of it. From that day on, we became a couple. God got him ready for me at the right time. Only God knows our needs. I'm so grateful to have had Michael in my life because we loved each other. His only concern was to make sure that I had everything I needed. We brought joy, love and support to each other.

THE YEAR 2020

The word people used to describe this year was unprecedented; they were referring to the Covid 19 virus that, it was ravishing the country. For me, the word was unbelievable because, so much more happened. The Scripture I stood on was **First Corinthians 10:13** which says, *"No temptation has overtaken you except such as is common to man, but God is faithful who will not allow you to be tempted beyond what you are able, but with the temptation will also make a way of escape, that you may be able to bear it."*

Michael and I had plans. He was going to open a studio where he would live and work and have clients come by appointment. He was going to cut down the number of shows he does per year and the distance that he would travel to shows. My plan was to continue to market my book in hopes to eventually get picked up by traditional publishing company. Our travel plans were a cruise to the Panama Canal.

In January, I went to Philadelphia for my sister's mother-in-law's 100th birthday. When I returned, Michael picked me up from the airport and stayed a couple of days and had to leave to prepare for the Pan- African Film and Arts Festival.

It would take him about two weeks to prepare for the show. We talked every day about how the show was going. I went down to see him on the first Sunday of the show. Michael's creative juices were off the chart. He created shadow boxes and handmade all the instruments that he placed inside of them. His presentation was fabulous and everyone loved his artwork.

This show is long, time consuming and physically draining. It would take him about 3 to 4 days to recover from it. About a week after the show, Michael started to complain about tightness in his chest and stomach and said he just did not feel well. Later, he would tell me that his stool was black. I suggested he should go to the doctor and get checked out. Once he got to the doctor's office, they ran a number of tests and decided to put him in the hospital. He was 68 years old and had never been in the hospital.

I prayed for his healing and ask God to give me the strength to handle whatever he had in store for me. Due to the pandemic, I was not able to see him. One day he called and said that, "Tammy, who is a nurse, but did not work in the hospital" Tammy was there? I asked. He said, "Tammy is here". I said really?

Let me tell you about Tammy, she is my angel. I have no doubt about that. God sends her in my time of need. This time it was for Michael. He needed to see a familiar face at that time. to remind him that he was not alone. God uses Tammy to bring joy, help and comfort.

After running many tests, they diagnosed him with a form of cancer. That would end up being a misdiagnosis. After many more tests and 2 biopsies, DNA test and genetic testing. I was glad he was in the VA hospital, so he would not have to worry about insurance, and they continued to test until they found out what was wrong with him. He had a great team of doctors along with a wonderful care team. It was finally determined that he had a rare disease called amyloidosis.

It occurs when a rare protein changes shapes and builds up in the muscle and organs and prevents them from working properly. 50,000 people in the world get it per year. There is NO CURE. Immediately I researched everything about the disease. The word 'no cure' when I read that, I could not believe what I was reading.

Treatment was chemotherapy and a bone marrow transplant. The success of the treatment depended on how fast the disease progressed. Michael's own was hereditary and affected all of his organs. I could not imagine how Michael felt when they told him. My heart ached to be with him. He was given one to two years to live. I fell to my knees and wept all the strength came out of my body.

After his first chemo session he was okay until that night he was in so much pain. He got up and put his clothes and shoes on and said I need to go to the hospital. I cannot believe the incompetence that occurred. They did not give him the pain medication he needed to take home with him. For His remaining chemo session, he stayed in the hospital

We talked daily, I prayed and asked God for a miracle which I know God is able. Michael was put on the list for a bone marrow transplant. In March they told him that all treatment had been exhausted and he had six months to live because the disease had progressed so quickly. I said to God no miracles for him? My heart was broken, I hoped that we would spend the rest of our lives together.

I asked God to give me peace that surpasses all understanding. Michael had the following symptoms fatigue, glaucoma, swelling of his lower legs, gastrointestinal issues and erectile dysfunction. The disease takes a long time to be diagnosed because the symptoms resemble other diseases. It normally takes about two years for a person to be diagnosed. Michael's first symptoms appeared in 2018.

I called my girlfriend Keeley, to tell her about Michael. We prayed for his healing. She said that she would keep him in her prayers. She had just turned 47 years old on February 8. I met her when she was 25 years old. She was a mature, funny, kind and giving Christian woman. She owned a home and drove a gold Cadillac. The next week I called her to check in to see how she was doing. She did not return my call which was not like her.

Finally, I called again and the voice mail was full my last call to her was on March 25. In April I received a program of her obituary in the mail from her mother who lives in Oklahoma. Keeley had died on March 2. I fell to my knees and wept I did not believe it because no one told me.

In May, on Facebook in messages, a message from her nephew dated March 2nd at 10am saying;" Miss Kim, my aunt Keeley passed" It made me feel better knowing that someone tried to reach me. Her nephew knew where I lived but he did know my address or unit number. what happened? I was just with her. A week later, someone called me about her ex-husband, Marcel and said that he was so devastated at her funeral. He began to drink heavily and died from heart complications. Marcel helped me at my house with repairs. He was a good guy. The deaths kept coming and by the end of the year, 11 people and my dog were gone.

Michael was with me for 3 months I was his care taker. I was thankful for our time together. The first month he was his normal self. The second month, he started to sleep more and have less energy. He was on a lot of medication and I made sure that he took everything on time.

It was frustrating for him. One day I was in my office and he was down stairs with KJ. I heard a noise like something had fallen. I rushed down stairs to see what had happened. I said honey what happened? KJ was looking like he wanted to say momma something did happen. Michael just said "Kim, you have to fix the cable". I pulled on the tv stand to try to keep from falling.

As I got closer to him, he had a cut above his eye and I took care of it. From that point on, I had his walker for him to get around in. He told me that was his second fall. I called his son who was still in town from Texas and the hospice company to discuss taking him to the hospital and everyone agreed, even Michael.

The day that I went to visit him, they were working on him because his blood pressure was low. That scared me. The nurse said, "don't worry, we will take you to a room to wait until he is stabilized and then come got you later". They gave us some time alone. I got as close as I could and hugged and kissed him and told him that I loved him and thanked him for being so good to me.

On July 28, I took KJ for his walk and on our way home, we had to pass a home owner who was standing in the garage with 2 pit bulls. As we passed, KJ went toward them, I pulled but his lease and his collar came off and the dogs grabbed him and had him in their mouths. I screamed and yelled, get them off of my dog. It was in the morning and everyone was at work. I ran up and down yelling; "help me, help me".

Then a man came running toward me saying, "My name is Alex your neighbour in unit 173. Let me help you". He was a God sent I was beside myself and could not think straight. He called the police and they took KJ to the hospital and Alex and I followed them and he brought me home.

When we got there, the policeman came out and said, "They do not do surgery here Ms. Blackwell. You want to talk to the doctor; he said your dog is too damaged and he would not have a good quality of life". I went in and put him down. It was supposed to be KJ and me when Michael died.

Michael died August 11th on that day a friend sent me a text reminding me with this question,

Who is God to you?
God is my everlasting father
God is my source
God is my Prince of peace
God is my Redeemer
God is my restorer
God is my friend

God is my refuge
God is my Prince of peace
God is my healer
God is my Lord of lords

God will never leave me nor forsake me and he is always there. That lifted my spirit and comforted me. My niece, Dawn, wrote a beautiful statement that said it all on Facebook.

"Aunt Kim, you two are, were, and will always be the living testimony of God's gifts compatibility and team work in love. I know your heart hurts by his departure. Keep focused on how wonderful it has been to be graced by a love like him. Not many humans never ever experienced. May Michael rest in paradise, carrying with him the joy you two experienced together on earth".

THE HUNT FOR MY FURRY FRIEND

It has been lonely without KJ and Michael but I have great friends that I talk to every day. I'm working on forgiving myself for blaming myself for KJ's death. I will get there as soon as I get another dog. I never thought it would take so long it has almost been a year that I have been looking.

I wanted to work with the rescue organization so that I can find out more information about the dog. I'm spoiled because KJ was such a great dog, he was three years old when I got him house trained, loved going for walks and was independent. He could stay at home alone without being in a cage. I was looking for a male little dog when grown would not be more than 25 pounds, they would like going for walks.

I had expanded my breeds to poodles pugs, Shin Tzu, and Pomeranians. Some of the dogs' profiles were funny. Here are a few. Auston a Shin Tzu mix is a special needs dog seven years old, 19 pounds medium energy, house trained, needs a secure yard a house no shared walls is blind but that does not stop him.

Copper-Chihuahua mix, two-year old, 8- pounds, separation anxiety, prefers women and wants to be the only dog. At first, it looked like it might work out but not good with men, now I cannot have that if I would like to have another man in my life.

Finally, glitter girl terrier Maltese mix, three years old, needs a calm home, with someone home often good so far and can give her the structure and boundaries and space she needs while she learns to trust her person. She does not like to be fussed over. Needs a yard and I'm looking to fuss over my dog she is not for me. I know that God will send the right dog to me.

HE IS ALWAYS THERE

Psalms 5:12 says, *"The angel of the Lord encamps all around those who fear him, and delivers them."*

I finally got an appointment to get the Covid 19 vaccine. The process was very challenging. The city of San Fernando offered the vaccinations at both parks. Las Palmas Park at505 S. Huntington Ave and San Fernando recreation Park.

I have lived in San Fernando for over 30 years and because I do not have children, I had never been to the parks. My appointment was at Las Palmas Park and I thought I knew where it was because on my daily walk, I pass Huntington Avenue. My appointment was at 10-am. so I decided to walk. As I set out, I came to Huntington Avenue and I made a left turn up the street.

The numbers were going up and not down. I saw a man and I asked him if he knew where the park was. He said, "Miss. you might want to try the other side." So, I turn around and went back and cross the street in the opposite direction. As I'm walking, I'm looking at the numbers; they were going up and it did not say South.

Then I get to a cul-de-sac and there's no park in sight. I turned around and went back. I saw a lady. I said, "excuse me, do you know where Las Palmas Park is?" Before I leave my home each day, I set my angels out about me. I told her I had a vaccination appointment there. She said, yes, I just got my vaccination and took my mother and father.

We got it at San Fernando recreation Park. She said that was closer. I said, I need to go where my appointment is. She said that, Park is on the other side by the railroad tracks. She said, "I work from home, I can take you?" she said. As I was leaving the house, I asked God to use me to help someone in need. I told her that every day I set my angels encamped about me before I go walking.

I told her that she was my angel for today. We walked back to her house which was close. I took a mental note of her address and the car license plate number and she drove me to the park. She said Kim, if you need a ride home, just give me a call if I'm in the middle of something I'll come get you when I'm done. Her name was Delilah. I said thank you so much but I think I'll be able to walk home from there.

When I got to the park, it was a long line. It took about an hour she called me right before I got finished. She said, "Kim are you finished yet?" I told her I just got done. she said, I'll be right there to pick you up and take you home. I said that's not necessary she said no I'll be there to come and get you wait for me. She came and took me home. She said, "Kim, if you ever need any help just give me a call, I will be glad to help you".

In my spirit I thought that she was a good person so I was not afraid. God is so merciful there are still wonderful and kind people out there. When I got home, I called everyone to tell them of my good news story. Michael had been in the hospital for two weeks due to Covid 19, so no one could visit him. One day, we were talking on the phone and he said Tammy is here. Tammy is a nurse but did not work in the hospital she just happened to be there that day. I said, "Tammy is there?" he said yes. I could hear the smile in his voice. Michael needed to see a familiar face in that moment.

Finally, the day KJ was killed by the pit bulls, my neighbor Alex, who I had never meant. God sent him to be the level headed person to help me because I was so traumatized. He called the police, took me to the hospital and brought me home. He continues to check on me today.

Conclusion

As I walk this faith-walk every day, the word of God becomes clearer to me. This Scripture says it all; Ephesians 1:18, *"The eyes of your understanding being enlightened, that you may know what is the hope of his calling, what is the richest of the glory of his inheritance in the saints."*

Genesis 1:22 states, *"God bless them and said be fruitful and multiply. For years I thought since I did not have children that I had not fulfilled God's desire for my life."* Then, I heard a message from an elder at my church in 2019 and the title of the message was "the seed on the inside". He said that God has not sent anyone to this earth empty. God has put a seed on the inside of us to be what he wants us to be. As we live this life, we are discovering our purposes and our destinies.

The seed that he placed in me is the desire to help others. When I look back on my life that has been the common denominator in everything I have done. I cannot tell you how powerful that message was to me.

I still listen to it today. Jeremiah 29:11 says "For I know the thoughts that I think toward you says the Lord, thoughts of peace not of evil, to give you a future and a hope." I give God all the praise, glory, honor and Thanksgiving for giving me life after stroke. I look forward to a long healthy life as I continue to grow in the word of God while strengthening my faith throughout all of Life's experiences.

Kim Blackwell a child of the living God.

Acknowledgments

She thanks her mother, Mildred Cowan and her sister, Vernice Wooden for their words of encouragements when she said that she was going to write another book.

She thanks her friends for being there for her. Some individuals she talks to daily and others that are there when she needs them. Brenda, Sharon, Sheri, Tammy, Brigitte, Randy, Rhonda, Joslyn, Geraldine, Ella and Anna. She wants to thank Sheila Atkins for holding her accountable to make sure that she finishes the book.

APPENDIX 1

Scriptures She Confessed Daily

Isaiah 55:11
So shall my word be that goes from out of my mouth, it shall not return to me void, but it shall accomplish what I please and it shall prosper in the thing for which I sent it.

Jeremiah 29: 11
For I know the thoughts that I think towards you, says the Lord, thoughts of peace and not of evil to give you a future and a hope

Proverbs 3;5-6
Trust in the Lord with all your heart, and lean not on your own understanding, in all your ways acknowledge him, he shall direct your paths.

Joshua 1 :9
Be strong and of good courage, do not be afraid for the Lord your God is with you wherever you go.

Psalm 91:2
I will say of the Lord, he is my refuge and my fortress my God in him I will trust.

Phippians 4:13
I can do all things through Christ who strengthens me.

2nd Timothy 1 ;7
God has not given us a spirit of fear but of power, of love and of a sound mind

APPENDIX 2

WORSHIP SONGS

James Cleveland

God Is

Laura Daigle Rescue

Travis Greene

Make A Way

Jeremy Camp

Out Of My Hands

Tauren Wells

Known

Danny Gokey

Wanted

CeCe Wining

I Believe for It

APPENDIX 3

PHOTOS

Paula and Kim at book signing.

Kim's book signing on March 10, 2018.

60th birthday New Orleans.

September 18 ,19 accidentan , interview.

Monterey Jazz Festival.

Entrepreneurial women of faith (2019).

My Dog; Princess.

Michael and Kim became couple in 2011.

National museum of African history and Culture.

Michael Phelps Art-works.

In Memory of
Michael Phelps

www.ingramcontent.com/pod-product-compliance
Lightning Source LLC
Chambersburg PA
CBHW031240120626
46545CB00003B/1205